Original title:
Bubbles in the Blue

Copyright © 2025 Creative Arts Management OÜ
All rights reserved.

Author: Theodore Sinclair
ISBN HARDBACK: 978-1-80587-341-9
ISBN PAPERBACK: 978-1-80587-811-7

Gleams of the Infinite

In the sky's bright grin so wide,
Float the giggles without pride.
Bouncing, skipping, up they soar,
Chasing dreams to the ocean's floor.

Laughter dances with the tide,
As silly fish do take a ride.
They tickle the feet of clouds above,
In this realm of whimsy and love.

Echoes Beneath the Surface

Waves are whispering jokes in jest,
With rubbery banter—oh, what a fest!
Ticklish bubbles tease the fray,
Sunkissed giggles drift away.

Perched on splashes, we find our glee,
While skimming through the wild sea.
Laughter's echoes swirl and twirl,
In watery realms where giggles unfurl.

Freedom in the Gentle Drift

Drifting on whimsies, light and free,
The tides invite us for a spree.
Silly shenanigans on a wave,
It's a joyous splash—so bold, so brave.

With a flip and a glide, the laughs unfold,
Bantering with seagulls, none too bold.
In this floating realm, we dance and sway,
Chasing the sunshine at the end of the day.

Celestial Playthings

Stars tumble down from the sky so vast,
Bouncing like marbles, they fly by fast.
Chuckling comets leave trails of light,
In their playful game that lasts all night.

Planets wink, and moons make faces,
Creating a carnival in cosmic spaces.
With every twinkle, a smile takes flight,
In this jolly dance of pure delight.

Whispers of the Sky

Up in the air, they wiggle and sway,
Glorious orbs at the end of the day.
Chasing a breeze, tickled with cheer,
Floating along, with nothing to fear.

They giggle and dance, round and round,
Casting soft shadows upon the ground.
With every new drift, a chuckle or two,
Life's little jesters, in skies so blue.

Floating Orbs of Joy

Tiny balloons on a playful spree,
Sailing through laughter, wild and free.
Each plop and a bounce, a giddy delight,
Chasing the wind under sun's golden light.

What are they thinking? Who knows for sure,
Maybe just giggles that drift and endure.
A hop, skip, and jump in the midday ray,
Silly little wonders that dance and play.

Celestial Drift

Wobbling wisps in a sky full of glee,
Tickled by breezes, just you and me.
Round and around in a frothy parade,
Jovial jesters all set to invade.

They slide through the clouds, oh what a sight,
A ballooning ballet in dazzling light.
Giggling whispers echo the cheer,
These wobbly travelers, what fun they steer!

Azure Echoes

In a sea of laughter, they wink and gleam,
Shimmering souls in a whimsical dream.
Twisting and turning, a frothy affair,
Joyful companions without a care.

They bounce up high, catching rays in flight,
With each little jiggle, they steal the light.
Chortles and chuckles as they dance on by,
Whimsical wonders in the vast, wide sky.

Skybound Simplicity

Up above, the laughter flows,
A dance of joy, where whimsy grows.
Floaty dreams in the light of day,
Chasing troubles far away.

Jolly shapes in the azure dome,
Whispers of giggles call me home.
With each bounce, the world seems bright,
A giggling heart takes joyful flight.

Effervescent Echoes

Frothy whispers rise and fall,
Each splatter sings, a merry call.
Waves of cheer that tickle the spine,
In the splash, the world aligns.

Laughter dances on the breeze,
Painted smiles amidst the trees.
Joyful ripples, a playful chase,
Every glance brings a silly face.

Transcendent Ripples

Wobbly forms in the sunny air,
Jokes float past without a care.
Each splish-splash a wink or tease,
Life's a game that aims to please.

Giggling waves and a cheeky grin,
With every bounce, let the fun begin.
Silly moments glide and swirl,
In this dance, let laughter unfurl.

Chasing Reflections

Silly shadows play on high,
As if the clouds too want to fly.
Mirrored smiles on the sparkling ground,
In the whimsy, joy is found.

A splash of color, a twist of fate,
Laughter bubbles, never late.
Each tiny splash, a moment to seize,
In this world, it's just a tease.

Tranquility's Ethereal Coating

Floating on the wavy crest,
With giggles lost in sunshine's nest.
A dance of glimmers, oh so sweet,
Where laughter's tickle finds its beat.

A dolphin flips, a splashy cheer,
While jellybeans swim, oh so near.
With frothy crowns of silly white,
Life's a joke in joyful flight.

A Sea of Shimmering Dreams

Whimsical waves with smiles so wide,
Rolling in laughter, let's take a ride.
Fish in tuxedos, waving hello,
They know the secrets we wish to know.

Stars of the ocean, sparkling bright,
Tickling our toes with pure delight.
A giggle here, a bubble there,
In the world where dreams float in air.

Whimsies in the Aquatic Expanse

Octopus juggling, what a sight!
With jellyfish tangoing, oh so light.
A sea cucumber's silly dance,
Makes every fish take a last chance.

With seahorses in tiny shoes,
They prance and twirl, no time to lose.
The underwater fairies, full of glee,
Share giggles and grins as they swim free.

Vapors Painting the Sky

With puffy clouds like cotton candy,
The winds blow softly, sweet and dandy.
A rainbow's arch, a cheeky grin,
Where dreams take shape, let joy begin.

Hiccups of laughter, a twist in air,
As vapors swirl in a light affair.
Chasing the giggles that drift nearby,
In a whimsical world up high.

Drenched by Azure Euphoria

Splash of joy in the sky,
Chasing droplets that fly.
Giggling as they pop, oh dear,
Like tickling toes of summer cheer.

Waves of laughter, wiggly fun,
Sunny faces, everyone.
Jump in puddles, make a splash,
Life's a game, go on and dash.

Floating dreams on bright delight,
Twinkling sparkles, oh what sight!
Chasing shadows of the day,
Wear a smile, come what may.

With a whoosh, they dance and dive,
Silly antics come alive.
In our hearts, the joy runs wild,
Life's a circus, we're the child.

Transitory Thoughts on Vapor Trails

A swirl of giggles in the air,
Clouds of laughter everywhere.
Witty whispers, soft and light,
With a chuckle, take your flight.

Skimming past on lightened feet,
Catch a joke, oh what a treat.
In the breeze, ideas bloom,
Silly thoughts make hearts resume.

Fluttering visions, fleeting smiles,
Zany moments stretch for miles.
Wobble here, then twist around,
In this frolic, joy is found.

As the twilight paints the sky,
Whimsy flows, oh me, oh my!
Dance along this vibrant stream,
Every chuckle fuels a dream.

Elysian Waters of Light

In a river of soft giggles,
Sunbeams dance, the laughter wiggles.
Splashes echo, joy so bright,
Every ripple sparks delight.

Round we go, a twist, a turn,
In this game, we laugh and churn.
Tickles tickled under the sun,
Hold on tight, it's all in fun.

With a pop, the joy erupts,
All around us, fun's construct.
Silly faces, silly games,
In this chorus, no one blames.

Navigating through the cheer,
In these waters, have no fear.
Splash and giggle, float away,
Life's a merry, silly play.

Harmony of Reflections in Tide

Ripples play with sunny beams,
Every moment bursts with dreams.
Flip and flap, a playful sight,
As we shimmer in the light.

Painted smiles on wavy streams,
Joyful laughter bursts at seams.
Let's skip stones and chase the breeze,
Forget the worries, just feel ease.

Flip-flops clatter on the shore,
Silly dances, let's explore.
Matching giggles with each stride,
In this echo, we abide.

Reflections spark with glee anew,
Carried forth by skies so blue.
As we leap and splash so high,
Every moment, a laughter nigh.

Gelid Horizons of Liquid Glass

In a world where splashes cheer,
Children laugh, with joy sincere.
Chasing swirls that dance in flight,
They burst like dreams in pure delight.

Gleaming orbs escape the ground,
Wobbling, wobbling, round and round.
A slippery slide of liquid jest,
In this frolic, they are the best.

With a twist and a leftward spin,
They giggle softly, let the fun begin.
Each glint reflects their playful bliss,
What a sight, that jolly kiss!

So come and join this silly race,
With laughter echoing, find your place.
For in this land of joyous play,
The liquid joy is here to stay!

Whirls of Light in Vast Skies

Dizzy spirals float above,
Like lost balloons that dance and shove.
They tickle clouds with a glittered tease,
While sunbeams scoop like tasty cheese.

Flying high with giddy cheer,
Each one peeks like a tiny seer.
A wink, a pop, oh what a sight,
They vanish fast, oh, what a fright!

Chasing giggles, round they go,
Racing shadows down below.
With every twist, a playful flip,
On this merry, frothy trip.

In the sky, they weave their dance,
Making skies a fun-filled prance.
For in this wonder, wild and wide,
Laughter bubbles, nothing to hide!

The Poetry of Gentle Ripples

Whispers ripple in the stream,
Where fishy friends go on a beam.
A plop, a splash, oh what a tease,
They giggle softly, float with ease.

From stone to stone, they leap along,
A serenade in liquid song.
Each gentle wave will kiss the shore,
Creating chuckles, oh, so sore.

With every swirl, a jest unfolds,
In silver glints, a tale retolds.
They sway and sway, what fun they bring,
The water's laughter starts to sing.

So let's take dip into this play,
Where every splash will lead the way.
For nature spins her silly lines,
And here we find our joyful signs!

Floating Chords in Aquatic Symphony

Plucky notes in waves arise,
Strumming chords beneath the skies.
With every bubble, laughter rings,
As merry fish perform their flings.

A symphony of giggles swell,
Where joyful splashes sing so well.
They twirl and twist with rhythmic grace,
In this liquid, lively place.

Echoes dance from shore to shore,
Each splash a note, we crave for more.
A chortle here, a whistle there,
In this water, fun hangs in the air.

So come aboard this merry tune,
Where glistening waves make light as a balloon.
For in this symphony of jest,
The ocean plays, and we are blessed!

A Symphony in Clear Waters

Floating whimsies dance with glee,
Chasing shadows, wild and free,
A splash of laughter, bright and bold,
In a world where joy unfolds.

Wobbly orbs in a wavy race,
Giggling giants join the chase,
Caught in ripples, they all fall,
Bouncing back, they heed the call.

Tickled by the sun's warm grin,
Round and round, they twist and spin,
Each one whispers tales of cheer,
Funny giggles fill the sphere.

With raucous squeaks, they tease the air,
Giddy moments everywhere,
They bubble up, then fizzle down,
In this aquatic, silly town.

Serene Effulgence

In the stillness of the tide,
Quirky visions take a ride,
Wobbly spheres float with flair,
Juggling thoughts without a care.

Chubby forms on waves entwined,
A gentle roll, a twist defined,
Rumbling laughter fills the glade,
In a wandering masquerade.

Sunbeams play a cheeky game,
Tickling surfaces, oh, how they came!
Round and round, a slippery chase,
In this dance, there's no disgrace.

As the evening shadows creep,
Silly sounds that make us leap,
Floating giggles, light and bright,
Chasing butterflies in flight.

Fragile Moments in the Great Expanse

Drifting whims in a wobbly scene,
Silly antics, a lively routine,
Chasing dreams, they bounce and glide,
With a splash, they turn the tide.

Up and down in a playful spin,
With every twist, they surely win,
Cheerful giggles from above,
Filling the air with a sprinkle of love.

Waves of chuckles, soft and round,
Embracing joy that knows no bound,
A fleeting moment in giggly flight,
Captured in laughter, pure delight.

Glistening orbs with cheeky flair,
Waving high in the warm air,
Floating freely, oh what a sight,
In this carnival of light.

Luminous Orbucular Journeys

Frolicking lights upon the bay,
Roundish forms at play today,
Jumping high with a cheerful hop,
Underneath the sun's bright top.

Bouncing here and bouncing there,
Silly songs fill the salty air,
Chasing echoes of glee and fun,
Splashes spark 'neath the laughing sun.

Mystic roundness in swirling tanks,
Mirthful smiles, playful pranks,
Bubbles wiggle, twist, and sway,
In a watery ballet display.

As day dips low and stars awake,
Oh the laughter, oh the shake!
Curious whispers in jolly tunes,
Join the dance 'neath the smiling moons.

Resonance in the Misty Air

A frog in a hat made of leaves,
Hopped on a wave, dancing with ease.
It blinked at a fish who wore a bow,
They laughed as the wind blew soft and low.

The clouds wore shoes that squeaked and squealed,
While sunlight tickled the grass that healed.
Giggles erupted from beyond the trees,
Where whispers of joy drifted like bees.

A cat on a cloud chased a bright kite,
The scene was so silly, it felt just right.
With hiccups and chuckles, the world spun around,
As laughter bubbled up from the ground.

In this place where giggles ignite,
Every silly moment felt so light.
With friendship afloat, and smiles that grow,
The fun never ceases, just look at the show!

The Color of Serenity

In a garden where rainbows often spin,
A dog in a suit danced with a grin.
Worms wore glasses, reading the sky,
While butterflies waltzed, oh my, oh my!

The tea was steeping in a pot with flair,
As gossiping clouds traded secrets rare.
A snail in a tux, oh what a sight,
Sipped lemonade with delight in the night.

A parrot recounted tales of old,
While the sun set, draping hues of gold.
Chirps of the crickets serenade the breeze,
As laughter took flight on each gentle tease.

This place painted smiles in every shade,
Where silliness bloomed, never to fade.
In the heart of wonder, all things are bright,
The color of joy, oh what a delight!

Silent Songs Beneath the Surface

In a pond where the shadows floated by,
A turtle with sunglasses winked at the sky.
Fish played hide-and-seek in the reeds,
While laughter erupted from tiny seeds.

A frog on a lily pad sang out of tune,
With crickets accompanying beneath the moon.
The waterbugs tapped in rhythmic delight,
Creating a show that felt just right.

A snail joined in with a shell that gleamed,
As bubbles rose up, and everyone dreamed.
The water danced, a symphony of cheer,
While friends all gathered, drawing near.

These songs of the deep, a whispery echo,
Bring smiles and giggles, oh, how they grow.
In the laughter beneath, where secrets reside,
The fun in the silence forever will glide!

A Spectrum of Floating Moments

On a day painted soft in pastel hues,
A squirrel juggled acorns, wildly amused.
With cotton candy clouds high in the air,
The scene felt like magic, beyond compare.

A raccoon in slippers danced on a tide,
While balloons drifted gently, side by side.
The grass wore a blanket of sparkling dew,
As laughter erupted, embracing the view.

With every twist, there's joy to be found,
In colors that shimmer, all around.
A ladybug twirled in a polka dot dress,
While the sun winked down, bestowing its bless.

Every moment floating, a treasure to keep,
In this funny realm, where giggles leap.
Here's to the dance of whimsical fun,
In the spectrum of laughter, we're never done!

A Tapestry of Light.

In a splashy swirl of glee,
Colors waltz with light so free.
A polka-dot parade on the sea,
Tickled by waves, laughing with me.

The sun plays tricks, a dance of rays,
It juggles shades in wobbly ways.
With giggles bright, the ocean sways,
As sun-kissed foam joins in the frays.

Floaties all around, the sights are sweet,
Silly shapes in a bubbly meet.
The seagulls join in, shuffle their feet,
And cheeky crabs clap to the beat.

In this lively realm, we lose our cares,
Making wishes on jellyfish flares.
Each splash a burst of giggly airs,
Crafting joy beyond compare.

Whispers of Aquatic Dreams

Down where the silliness reigns supreme,
Fish wear hats in a fanciful scheme.
They frolic and wiggle, less like a team,
While seaweed giggles, floats downstream.

Pufferfish puff in a playful jest,
Shaking their fins like they're at a fest.
Every flip and twirl puts smiles to test,
In this dreamy world, we're truly blessed.

Starfish twirl in a slow-motion dance,
As turtles plot their next goofy prance.
Each sea pogos in a whimsy trance,
While crabs tap out their crabby romance.

With whispers of joy, the ocean sings,
A chorus of laughter; oh, the joy it brings!
In the deep blue, all mischief springs,
Surfing silly waves on outlandish swings.

Floating on Celestial Waves

Up in the sky, where clouds wear crowns,
The waves below wear silly frowns.
A dolphin juggles, flipping around,
While laughing otters slide down to towns.

In twilight twinkles, the sea folks cheer,
As starfish toss letters, full of good cheer.
Whales whistle tunes, what a sight so dear,
While mermaids spread giggles far and near.

Floating high on a giggle spree,
Pelicans dance on the briny tea.
The world is a stage, watch them decree,
That joy is the ticket for wild and free.

With merry sounds that bloom and glide,
We ride the tide on this joyful ride.
Each splash and giggle, we wear with pride,
In this whimsical realm, we will abide.

The Dance of Liquid Orbs

In a bounce and sway, they rise and fall,
Round and round, like a merry ball.
They tickle the toes, they splash at all,
While giggling fish do the liquid crawl.

Each droplet sings a-chortling rhyme,
In silly circles, they dance in time.
Life's a grand show, a grandiose mime,
Where every bubble bursts in sublime.

Octopuses twist in a goofy spree,
With arms all akimbo, as wild as can be.
They paint the water with jolly glee,
As laughter bubbles, oh joyfully free.

In this ripple world, the fun won't cease,
As every splash brings a wave of peace.
Join in the dance, bring your own fleece,
In a liquid realm where we're all released.

Liquid Lullabies

In a glassy sea, a dance unfolds,
Frothy giggles, secrets told.
Laughter bounces, round and light,
Sipping joy under the sun so bright.

Whispers tickle the surface thin,
Wobbly wonders make us grin.
Each splash a joke, a merry prank,
A toast to bubbles, we raise our tank.

Frothy dreams in a fizzy whirl,
Pirouettes of laughter, watch them twirl.
A fizzy farewell, a cheer, a cheer!
In this playful wave, we have no fear.

So here we float, with glee and flair,
In our wild ride through the watery air.
Each sip a song, a melody sweet,
In liquid lullabies, we find our beat.

The Choreography of Air

Tiny dancers in the bright sunlight,
Twirling and spinning, what a sight!
They slip and slide in a twisty spree,
A ballet of glee, living free.

Fluffy puffs chase their own tails,
Every jump sings like joyous tales.
With every float, a wink, a wink,
In the playful air, we gently sink.

Ticklish breezes play tag with the sky,
Bumping and bouncing, oh me, oh my!
Each gust a laugh, a wink so sly,
In this whimsical world, we simply fly.

So let's giggle in this airy waltz,
With every breath, we break the vaults.
A choreography that won't stop,
In the dance of air, we hop and bop!

Spheres of Serenity

Round and jolly, they travel high,
Floating fluffy like clouds in the sky.
Wobbling here and then rolling there,
Each little sphere a belly laugh to share.

Glowing colors, a carnival show,
Popping giggles as they go.
A wink of mischief in every glance,
Inviting all to join the dance.

They spin and twirl, playfully wild,
Like mischief-makers, oh so mild.
In this realm, we lose our frown,
With every round, we're up, not down.

Oh what fun we have in sight,
In serendipity's playful light.
As they bounce and soar, together we cheer,
In spheres of joy, we shed our fear.

Delicate Floating Wishes

Wishful dreams on a soft breeze,
Pleading for laughter, oh pretty please.
They dance like whispers, light and fair,
Eager to float, they fill the air.

With a pitter-patter, they leap from hand,
Spinning stories, unplanned and grand.
Every little wish a seasonal joke,
A giggle that glimmers—a soft poke.

They bob and weave, around they glide,
In a joyful frolic, we take the ride.
With a pop and a sizzle, they tumble down,
Turning our frowns around, around!

So raise your dreams to catch the fun,
In delicate bubbles, we all run.
With wishes afloat, we dance the night,
In the shimmering glow, everything feels right.

Enchanted Airborne Dots

In a sky of giggles, they float and sway,
Chasing the sunshine, they twirl and play.
Wobbling like jelly, they burst with cheer,
Tickling the clouds, they disappear.

With a pop and a fizzle, they dance and spin,
Painting the air, where the giggles begin.
Silly little creatures, so round and bright,
Telling the stars to laugh out loud tonight.

In the realm of wonder, they tease the breeze,
Catching surprises with amazing ease.
Little orbs of joy, oh what a sight,
Frolicking freely, oh what delight!

They whisper secrets, full of delight,
In a tangle of laughter, they take flight.
With every burst, new stories arise,
A carnival of dreams that fills the skies.

Glimmers of Light and Laughter

A sprinkle of laughter floats through the air,
Radiating joy, without a care.
Tiny spheres of whimsy, they roll and glide,
Chasing after smiles, heartbeats collide.

Juggling rainbows as they wobble around,
Creating a circus above the ground.
Each spark a giggle, a teasing delight,
They dance with the day, igniting the night.

In pockets of sunlight, they twinkle and shine,
Giggles erupt, oh how they align.
With a zip and a zoom, they float on by,
Eager to catch every wild, silly sigh.

As daylight dims and moonbeams play,
These trivial wonders just won't fade away.
Seeping in shadows, they twirl and chase,
Leaving trails of delight, filling up space.

Luminous Fancies

In a swirl of delight, they bounce and bob,
Glittering orbs from a whimsical job.
They twist and whir, with a chuckle so sweet,
Spreading the joy, oh what a treat!

Floating along on a breeze full of giggles,
Jiggling and jostling, in joyous wiggles.
With every soft crash, a chuckle released,
In such silly antics, their joy has increased.

Through holes in the clouds, they shimmer and shine,
Bouncing on sunbeams, it's simply divine.
A circus of laughter, they pop and they play,
Winking at the world in their own funny way.

Like playful sprites, they scatter and spin,
Mischief and giggles wrapped up in their skin.
With bright little hues, they twinkle so bright,
Making the mundane feel incredibly right.

Fragments of a Daydream

In a splash of color, they tumble and tease,
Giggling softly with every soft breeze.
Tiny droplets of dreams, oh how they shine,
Daring reality to cross the line.

Each little orb holds a tale so grand,
Floating together, perfectly planned.
They tease the edges of laughter's embrace,
In a whimsical dance, they find their place.

With a burst of delight, they rise and they fall,
Hilarity wrapped in a shimmering thrall.
Caught in a moment, suspended in time,
In a world where the silly is simply sublime.

On a raft of joy, they drift through the air,
Painting the skies with a splash of flair.
In the warmth of a giggle, they glow and sway,
Fragments of a dream that refuses to stray.

Nature's Delicate Jewel Box

In the garden, a dance begins,
Small orbs of joy, laughter spins.
They float like dreams, with giggles bright,
A rainbow of bounce, pure delight.

Petals play tag, their colors gleam,
Chasing the sun like a child's dream.
Nature's laughter, a playful tease,
Crafting rhythms in the breeze.

Droplets wear crowns of sunlight's cheer,
Winding through blushing blooms, oh dear!
With every jiggle, a chuckle rings,
As nature's charm on sweet joy clings.

So let's swirl in this joyful array,
Where giggles bounce and colors play.
In a box of jewels, nature's embrace,
Find laughter bright in every place.

Celestial Cherubs in Clear Waters

Up in the sky, the fluffy flies,
Scroll like paper, with giggly sighs.
Each little splat of laughter spills,
Painting the waves with tickled thrills.

Cherubs giggle as they dive and dart,
A splash of joy spills from their heart.
With each silky glide, they tease and play,
Creating ripples, in a joyous ballet.

Fish wiggle, wondering what's the fuss,
While splashing friends create a buzz.
Their shimmer twinkles in a watery waltz,
As laughter dances, it never halts.

Waves winks back as they rise and swell,
Carrying stories they're eager to tell.
In this watery wonder, joy flows free,
Fun's the anthem of the sea.

The Crystal Cascade

A playful rush down the mountainside,
Where giggles tumble and splashes glide.
Clear droplets leap, a comic ballet,
Dancing in sync, they twirl and play.

The rocks chuckle as the streams engage,
Nature's humor, a lively stage.
Waterballs bounce, in the sunlight's glow,
Making laughter wherever they go.

Each twist and turn, a giggly surprise,
As the cascade sparkles like mischievous eyes.
With each little jump, a bubble of glee,
Carving a path, so wild and free.

So join in the frolic, the rush, and the cheer,
Where each crystal laugh is a gift sincere.
In this waterfall of joy, we find our way,
Amidst the chuckles of a bright sunny day.

Gentle Horizons of Whispering Waves

Horizons stretch where the sea does play,
Whispering stories in a breezy sway.
Waves crack a smile, as they fold and curl,
Each splash a secret, like a soft, sweet pearl.

With the tide's giggle, they tease the shore,
Calling on friends to laugh and explore.
Sand castles wiggle with each tiny crash,
As children's laughter springs forth with a splash.

In the dip and rise, the fun flows free,
Where horizons smile at you and me.
A medley of joy, bright and light,
Under the sun, it feels just right.

These gentle whispers tell tales so true,
Of every day's fun, awaiting for you.
So listen closely to the waves' own tune,
Fun-filled adventures from morning to noon.

Journeying Through Fluid Realms

In the realm where giggles flow,
Fish wear crowns, putting on a show.
Jellybeans swim, bouncing in waves,
Chasing after seaweed, oh how it braves!

Sponges dance in a silly trance,
Winking at octopi with a cheeky glance.
Ticklish tides tease every fin,
In this world where whimsy begins!

Mermaids sing with voices so high,
Making the starfish dance and fly.
Seahorses twirl in a ballet grand,
As laughter ripples through the sand.

With laughter bubbles in every crest,
Under the waves, we find our nest.
Plucking joy from the glee-filled sea,
Forever laughing, just you and me.

Dreams Captured in Water's Embrace

In liquid dreams where laughter glows,
Kangaroos dive, how silliness flows!
Turtles laugh in a spinning race,
Who knew the sea could be such a place?

Rainbows swim by on watery swings,
Giggling as they sprout tiny wings.
Seashells gossip, it's quite a sight,
Telling tales under the moonlight.

A narwhal prances, a tutu it wears,
Guess it felt fancy with all of its flares.
Waves tickle clams in a friendly hug,
While dolphins snicker, content to shrug.

With laughter dancing like sun on the sea,
Every splash tells a story, just so free.
In these watery dreams where humor thrives,
Joy and frolic, oh how it jives!

Glittering Currents and Celestial Pleasantries

The river laughs as it winds away,
Jellyfish giggle, bright in their sway.
Stars sprinkle twinkles atop the splash,
As fishes tease, oh, they are brash!

A chorus of bubbles sings in delight,
Tickling turtles through the underwater night.
Each ripple brings laughter, a cheeky nudge,
As aquatic friends form a playful grudge.

Frogs in hats jump through golden light,
Making the crabs laugh, oh what a sight!
The waters sparkle with mischief and glee,
Turning every moment into a spree.

In this dance of currents, joy takes its flight,
Filling the ocean with pure delight.
So catch the giggle, hold it near,
In this sparkling sea, let laughter steer!

The Mirage of Floating Spheres

In a world of whimsy, spheres take flight,
Round and jolly, they bounce through the night.
Dancing with glee, they roll all around,
A parade of laughter, joy is found!

They drift on currents, soft and sweet,
Whispering secrets with every heartbeat.
Puffing marshmallows as they float by,
While cotton candy clouds tickle the sky.

A squirrel in a bubble, what a surprise!
Spinning like a top, oh how it flies!
Each twirl is a giggle, each swirl is a cheer,
Laughter with each bounce, nothing to fear!

With visions of floating and laughter in tow,
We join in the fun, just letting it flow.
In this mirage, our spirits take wing,
Celebrating the joy that our hearts can bring!

Shimmering Dreams

In a realm where giggles fly,
Wobbly orbs drift and sigh.
With each pop, they burst with glee,
Making wishes wild and free.

Laughter dances on the breeze,
Chasing sweetness, teasing tease.
They glow in hues of bright delight,
Playful spirits in the light.

Round and round, they twist and spin,
As silly thoughts begin to grin.
Floating whimsies, oh so light,
In this world, we take flight.

So join the fun, don't hesitate,
Commotion wrapped in laughter's state.
A shimmering dream, don't let it slip,
Grab a friend and take a trip!

Ephemeral Spheres

Tiny globes with frothy cheer,
Laughing softly, always near.
They giggle gently, mightily roll,
Swirling stories, heart and soul.

Each one sways with a silly flair,
Bobbing high with splendid air.
Catch them quick, a fleeting chase,
Watch them twirl in a merry race.

They hold the secrets of pure delight,
In a whimsical, merry flight.
Each pop is a joke, each float's a pun,
The game of joy has just begun!

At sunset's glow, they join the fray,
Dancing stars, the night's ballet.
With a chuckle, they wink and sigh,
Ephemeral friends that zip on by.

Dancing on the Water's Surface

Skimpy silks on shimmering waves,
Frolicking charms, our laughter saves.
Chasing ripples in a merry round,
In this folly, let joy abound.

Wobbly figures twirl and tease,
Sipping giggles like gentle breeze.
Each leap a jest, a splash of fun,
With silly antics 'til day is done.

Jump on the lake, paint it bright,
The world's a stage, our hearts alight.
With every plop, a sparkle winks,
In this dance, the heart just thinks.

So float along, and join the throng,
With chuckles loud, we can't go wrong.
Each wave a laugh, each splash a song,
In this frolic, we all belong.

Iridescent Fantasies

Colors spark, a glitter parade,
In this realm, we've fearless played.
Cupped in palms, they wiggle and twirl,
Each vibrant flick, a joyful whirl.

Jests in the air, oh what a show,
Tickling the sky, they ebb and flow.
With silly leaps, they rise and dive,
In this whimsy, we come alive.

Round the pond, giggles abound,
Froggy friends leap up and down.
With hearts so light, we take our stance,
Caught in this whimsical dance.

So hold your breath and let them fly,
A dreamlike world in the blink of an eye.
With every pop, roar with delight,
These fantasies dance through the night.

The Joy of Weightless Wanderings

Floating high in happy air,
Twisting, turning without a care.
Giggling seas of squishy delight,
Gravity's gone, oh what a sight!

Watch as friends take silly dives,
Chasing joy, where laughter thrives.
Upward spirals in silly play,
Bouncing dreams all day, hooray!

Wobbling like a jellybean,
Life is grand and oh so keen.
With a splash and twirl to see,
Freedom bubbles, wild and free!

Fleeting echoes, silly sounds,
In this realm where fun abounds.
Jump on out, don't stay confined,
Let the giggles fill your mind!

Crystal Serenade

Glittering spheres in a sunny dance,
Twinkling lights with a chance to prance.
Each twist and turn brings joyful cheer,
Floating marvels, we all cheer!

Twirling dreams like ice cream cones,
Silly laughter in playful tones.
Splashes of joy, oh what a sight,
In this sparkle, vibrant and bright!

With radiant giggles in the air,
Echoing happiness everywhere.
Life is a song, witty and clear,
Every note brings friends near!

Chasing whispers, laughter grows,
In this melody, how it flows.
In waves of joy, let's celebrate,
Sway with the fun, it's never late!

Sailing with Aqua Wishes

Wishing on sails where dolphins play,
Spinning dreams that drift away.
Tickling waters, what a ride,
Joyful hearts, can't be denied!

With laughter loud like thunder's clap,
A carefree world, a cosmic map.
Sailing free on a wavy spree,
Every splashy wave wants to be!

Whirling wishes on a gentle beam,
Surfing joy like a happy dream.
Wobbly hats and silly tunes,
Under the bright and giggling moon!

Here's to friends with raucous glee,
Setting sail on sweet jubilee.
Aboard this ship of fun and mirth,
Adventures spark where joy gives birth!

The Language of Liquid Light

Whispers float on shimmering beams,
Language spun from playful dreams.
Bubbling giggles twist and glide,
Liquid laughter, can't abide!

In dappled waves, where shadows peak,
Funny faces, they play hide and seek.
Chasing sparkles with feet aglow,
Laughter ripples, to and fro!

Every flicker gleams with cheer,
Echoes of fun, drawn near and dear.
In a world where bright lights dance,
Joyful rhythms put us in a trance!

Gleeful moments shared tonight,
In the glow of happy light.
So come along, let's take a flight,
To where the heart sings pure delight!

A Symphony of Spheres

Plump orbs afloat like silly dreams,
Chasing giggles on sunlit streams.
A plink and a plop, they dance with glee,
Making the clouds laugh and flee.

They bounce and they wobble, a jolly parade,
Twirling in air like a youthful charade.
What a sight, these plump little jesters,
Tickling the sky, loving their festers.

The wind joins the party, giving a shove,
As they tumble and twirl, all in good love.
With a splash and a pop, they craft their own tune,
Yodeling bright, beneath the swoon.

A grand spectacle, vibrant and strange,
In the vast, open world, they playfully range.
Like silly balloons at a whimsical fair,
Laughing and giggling, without a care.

The Dance of Light

Shimmering sprites in the sun's warm glow,
Wiggle and jiggle, putting on a show.
Each twist and turn, a riotous spree,
As laughter lights up in the air so free.

Flip-flopping around, in a dazzling race,
With a frolicsome bounce and a playful face.
Echoes of joy with each radiant leap,
Sprinkling delight as the shadows creep.

They twist through the air, like a merry band,
On droplets of laughter, so light and grand.
The sky wears a smile, the wind gives a cheer,
As the dance of bright orbs draws everyone near.

In this kaleidoscope of bright hues and fun,
The world seems to sparkle, a joyous run.
Catch the magic, let your spirit delight,
In the whimsical splash of the dance of light.

Skyward Reveries

Up in the heavens, where dreams take flight,
Puffy little orbs twirl day and night.
Each broken bubble a tale to be told,
Of starlit dances and joys we behold.

With a wink and a nod, they frolic so free,
Whispering secrets to the old sycamore tree.
Their laughter like whispers on a soft breeze,
Turning the mundane into a tease.

A cultural mash-up of giggles and glee,
Floating on wishes like a bright jubilee.
As they glide and they gleam, what a sight to see,
Their whimsical flight is pure jubilee.

So let your heart soar with each buoyant twist,
As they soar and spin in a playful tryst.
In the silent echo of laughter and cheer,
The sky holds their secrets, forever near.

Reflections in the Shallow

A mirror of joy, with ripples so wide,
Wobbling giggles as they glide and slide.
Tiny rainbows seemed to appear,
In every smirk of joy, clouds disappear.

The surface dances with mischievous flair,
Showing off secrets, with laughter to spare.
Jumping the puddles, each splish a thrill,
A party of whispers, hearts can't be still.

Each tiny trip brings a splash of delight,
Painting the water with colors so bright.
A carnival moment, caught in the now,
Keeping the laughter, as wrinkles endow.

In shallow reflections, joy leaps and bounds,
Echoing giggles in soft, playful sounds.
For every gleam holds a memory sweet,
A song in the distance—a playful retreat.

Serenity's Liquid Canvas

Floating dreams with giggles so bright,
Waves of laughter dance in delight,
Splashing colors in the gentle tide,
A canvas of joy where secrets hide.

Tickled by currents, we glide with glee,
Silly fish swim, just as carefree,
Gazing at clouds with silly grins,
As the playful tide invites us in.

With every dip, the air's alive,
Jokesters of nature, oh how we thrive,
Chasing reflections, we leap and spin,
In this joyous swirl, let the fun begin!

And as the sun dips, a wink goodbye,
We drift away on a pastel sky,
With laughter echoing, we ride the flow,
In serenity's art, giggles ever grow.

Enchanted Sail on Vast Horizons

Whimsical winds fill our laughter sails,
Chasing seagulls with whimsical tales,
Skimming across where silly dreams roam,
We find our adventure far from home.

Decks made of candy, the crew's all spry,
Tickling the waves, we zip and fly,
Pirates of fun on our frothy ride,
Giggles and grins, oh, what a tide!

Every splash a chuckle, every wave a cheer,
With jellybeans swirling, we disappear,
Sailing the skies in pastel regalia,
Where laughter's the rule, and joy's a failure!

Nightfall brings sparkles, a shimmering spree,
As pirates of laughter, forever we're free,
On enchanted waters, we shall remain,
With horizons of humor, we'll sail again.

Reflections on a Glassy Sea

Glimmering tides like a mirror's cheer,
Where silly thoughts and giggles appear,
Jumping fish share their jokes, oh so grand,
In this shiny world, fun is close at hand.

Laughter rises with each gentle swell,
Bouncing along in our merry shell,
Reflected smiles as bright as the sun,
In watery circles, we all become one.

Secrets ripple beneath the calm guise,
As we trade puns with the birds in the skies,
Floating on echoes, we spin and sway,
With each little splash, we giggle away.

The horizon giggles, a cosmic jest,
While shoreline friends are all on a quest,
In this glassy realm, let fun take charge,
With laughter as waves, life feels so large.

Dancing Lights in the Alkaline Air

Jumps of joy in the fizzy spray,
Colors of laughter party all day,
Fizzy tides dance under sunlight's gaze,
In this luminous haze, we twirl and blaze.

Giggling clouds bounce with a twist,
Winking raindrops make it hard to resist,
With every flicker, we laugh like kids,
In the playful air, all worries hid.

Carefree bubbles pop, a splendid sound,
With tiny splashes, our joy is profound,
Chasing the sparkles, hearts buoyant and bright,
In this whimsical swirl, we take flight.

As dusk settles down, the lights start to play,
Ushering smiles at the close of the day,
In the alkaline air where laughter cascades,
We'll dance with the stars, in jolly charades.

A Breath of Liquid Air

In a glassy world, we play,
Laughter rises, bright and gay.
Floating dreams, like jelly beans,
Pop! They vanish, giggles tease.

Whirling round in joyful spins,
Chasing light with cheeky grins.
Sips of joy in every drop,
Wishing this would never stop.

Tiny orbs in playful flight,
Dancing 'neath the morning light.
With a splash, we burst with cheer,
Raising our mugs, it's time for beer!

In this liquid, laughter flows,
Whimsy where our friendship grows.
A world where every sip's a thrill,
In this fun, we've had our fill.

Kaleidoscope of Floating Wishes

Colors swirl in merry chase,
Joyful smiles upon each face.
Wishing stars that bounce and play,
A giggle here, a laugh all day.

Fluffy clouds that tickle toes,
Look! A rainbow bends and flows.
Light as air, our voices ring,
We're the jesters of the spring.

Tiny wishes float and sway,
Popping up to steal the day.
With a wink, they swirl around,
Laughter is the sweetest sound.

Chasing dreams on puffy ground,
In this mirth, we are unbound.
A heart that's light, we'll fly so high,
On our hopes, we'll touch the sky!

Ephemeral Whispers at Dusk

As the sun dips down so low,
Whispers giggle, soft and slow.
In the twilight, shadows tease,
Light and laughter in the breeze.

Frothy waves with silly hues,
Dance around our merry news.
With a shush, we share a cheer,
The night's here, and fun draws near.

Twirling whispers fill the air,
A friendly tease, a playful dare.
In this moment, time stands still,
Belly laughs, what a thrill!

Ephemeral joys, fleeting fast,
Let's hold on, make this one last.
With every giggle, stars align,
In our hearts, a sparkle shines.

The Essence of Gentle Currents

Drifting dreams on water's smile,
Tickled feet will stay a while.
Naughty waves that splash and play,
Leading us on a cheeky way.

Nudging friends with teasing glee,
"Catch me if you can!" said we.
Glassy surfaces, laughter's song,
In this game, we all belong.

With a skip and somersault,
We dive in deep, it's not our fault!
Echoes ring like bellies shake,
Waves of joy, it's ours to take.

In currents swift, our spirits soar,
Chasing whimsy, craving more.
As night unfolds in shades of fun,
Together, we are never done.

Echoing Dreams by the Waterside

On the shore they giggle and sway,
Chasing their laughter, come what may.
A plop, a splash, the fish they tease,
Tickling the toes of the playful breeze.

With a wiggle, they dance on a wave,
Who knew the pond could be so brave?
A ripple of joy that leaps and bounds,
A jester's delight in watery sounds.

They patter and plink, a cheeky refrain,
Whirling in circles, doing it again.
Laughter erupts like the sun's bright rays,
Making mischief in delightful ways.

Splashing about in a carefree spree,
A world of wonders, just wait and see!
With each little pop, a smile is found,
Echoing dreams with a giggly sound.

The Palette of Quiet Waters

Colors collide in a playful scene,
Where ripples giggle, and the frogs convene.
Painted reflections, a winking game,
Dancing with shadows, never the same.

A plush little duck with a hat askew,
Quacking in tune as the light breaks through.
Splashes of laughter paint the air bright,
While a snail slow-dances, oh what a sight!

With brushes of fun, they color the day,
The canvas of chaos in their own way.
Each stroke is a chuckle, each splash is a sound,
In soothing waters, silliness abounds.

A riot of hues in the sun's warm kiss,
Whisked into laughter, a splash we can't miss.
Artistry weaves through both time and place,
The palette of giggles painted in grace.

An Ode to Floating Delights

In the stillness, a ripple awakes,
A hushed little dance, as laughter breaks.
Swirls of mischief on the sparkling crest,
With giggles afloat, they're truly blessed.

Like feathers they drift, with whimsical flair,
The sunlight winks through the strands of air.
Gentle as whispers, absurdly serene,
Every little splash, a scene to be seen.

A frog in a top hat, so dapper and spry,
Leaps like a magician, oh my, oh my!
With a flick and a flop, he bows to the crowd,
And all of the water gets giggly and loud.

Jellybean ripples make silly shapes glow,
As fishy comedians put on quite a show.
In this giddy realm where delight is the king,
We laugh at the joys that afloat always bring.

Serendipity in the Glistening Surface

Oh, what a prankster the water can be,
Reflecting our smiles so playfully!
A splash of surprise, a wink and a grin,
The game is afoot, let the fun begin!

Droplets like diamonds, they scatter and play,
Skimming the top, then floating away.
Singing with ripples, they dance and they spin,
Joyful mischief, let the giggles begin!

A turtle in shades waves from the rim,
As dragonflies join in a whimsical hymm.
With each little twirl, the laughter expands,
In a kingdom of fun where silliness stands.

Here's to the wonders so light and so free,
Where every bright splash is a jubilee.
Beneath sunlit skies, let us jump and dive,
Embracing the joy, feeling so alive!

Tranquil Orbs in a Vast Expanse

In the sky, they dance and sway,
Round and bright, they steal the day.
With giggles soft, they float so high,
Chasing clouds, oh me, oh my!

A silly game, they rise and fall,
Like balloon animals at a ball.
Swirling, twirling in the light,
Turning day into sheer delight.

Each one wears a silly face,
Made of laughter, wrapped in grace.
Giggling whispers as they pop,
Who knew fun could never stop?

Oh, the joy as they collide,
Rolling merrily, side by side.
Laughter echoes in the air,
With no worries, just pure flair.

Celestial Thoughts on Liquid Clouds

Floating gently, round and sweet,
Drifting high, a tasty treat.
Caught in breezes, soft and light,
For giggles, it's a perfect flight.

They sizzle sassy with every glide,
Chasing dreams, no need to hide.
A wobbly world in cotton fluff,
Who knew the sky could be so tough?

With splashes of joy, they twist and twirl,
Like jelly beans in a happy whirl.
Each bounce a chuckle, every plop,
In the sunny air, they just won't stop.

Round the sun they laugh and tease,
Tugging at the playful breeze.
With every giggle, they ignite,
A universe of sheer delight.

Echoes of a Dreamy Horizon

On the edge of dreams, they gleam,
Floating softly, like a dream.
With a wink, they drift away,
Turning night into a play.

They bounce and peep, laughing loud,
Gathering joy like a happy crowd.
Silly whispers fill the air,
Chasing shadows, light as air.

In the twilight, their sparkle shows,
In rare colors, the laughter grows.
With each giggle, the stars align,
Encapsulated in pure design.

Through a lens of glee they glide,
Making mischief on the ride.
In the echoes, their joy is clear,
A fairy tale to make you cheer.

A Tapestry of Ethereal Mist

In a haze of giggles bright,
Dancing gently, oh, what a sight!
Fizzling softly through the gray,
Each twist and turn just wants to play.

A patchwork of laughter, tangled cheer,
Swaying with moves that draw you near.
Tickling noses with misty glee,
What a playful mystery!

Round and round, they flip and flop,
In a wacky whirl, they never stop.
Poking through the silly fog,
Creating magic like a dreamt-up dog.

With each burst, a chortle calls,
Bouncing off the softest walls.
In this mist, sweet laughter sings,
A tapestry of playful things.

Ribbons of Light on the Current

A dance of sparkles in midair,
The fish are laughing, flipping hair.
Swirling laughter, bright delight,
As colors weave, a playful flight.

With giggles echoing the stream,
The sunbeams bounce, a light dream.
A jolly choir from the shore,
While splashy jokes we all adore.

Each ripple sings a comical tune,
As shadows mingle, chase the moon.
The water winks, a cheeky glance,
Inviting all to join the dance.

In this giggly, shimmering show,
We float along, just let it flow.
Waves erupt in jest and cheer,
As we all burst with laughter here.

Driftwood and Dreams

A log that dreams of being grand,
Floats by with hopes, a wooden band.
It tickles toes and sways with glee,
A lazy pirate on the sea.

Seagulls squawk their silly songs,
While driftwood giggles, hums along.
It spins in circles, full of flair,
Its life a game, without a care.

Little crabs wear hats and shoes,
They waltz about, bring in the blues.
The tide, a jester, pulls them near,
While driftwood chuckles, never fear.

As waves and laughter crash and swirl,
Our dreams are caught in this grand whirl.
With every splash, a chuckle bright,
Driftwood laughs till the morning light.

The Wind's Favorite Plaything

A kite took flight, both big and bright,
It tickles clouds, a clear delight.
The wind just giggles, pulling tight,
As laughter soars into the night.

Little leaves join in the game,
They twirl around, forget the same.
With dandelions flying free,
The breeze is bursting, can't you see?

A hat that tumbles, twirls in play,
Chasing gusts, it runs away.
Oh what a riot, up so high,
The breeze is blushing as it flies.

So take a chance, let laughter ring,
In every gust, the joy we bring.
With tousled hair and hearts so light,
We dance with nature, a funny sight.

Luminescent Fantasies

In the night, glowworms gleam,
Lighting up a sparkly dream.
They giggle softly, dance in glee,
Painting darkness, oh so free.

A frog in shades of neon bright,
Croaks corny jokes, a funny sight.
The stars above can't help but grin,
As laugh lines dance upon their skin.

Mice with lanterns prance around,
In this comedy, joy is found.
With tiny hats and shoes that squeak,
Their silly antics make us weak.

The night is filled with mirth and cheer,
Where laughter echoes far and near.
In glowing worlds, we float and sway,
Embracing magic, come what may.

Glistening Waters Under Starlight

In the night, the splashes gleam,
Fish in tuxedos plot and scheme.
Giggles rise from the shallow shore,
As they dance, they ask for more.

Moonbeams play on puddles wide,
Frogs in hats take a slippery ride.
The crickets sing, a band in tune,
While turtles juggle beneath the moon.

A starfish takes a daring dive,
Swapping jokes, quite alive!
The water's laugh is a bubbling cheer,
As they frolic, without a fear.

With each splash, a riot of fun,
The night keeps rolling, never done.
Adventure awaits, let's not delay,
In these glistening waves, we'll play.

Soft Gales and Shimmering Spheres

Violet winds swirl round the pond,
Wishing to dance, and then they respond.
Marshmallows bounce on the gentle breeze,
All laughing madly, buzzing with ease.

The daisies blush in the playful air,
As delicate orbs float everywhere.
They trade silly stories, oh so light,
Hopping and bobbing, a whimsical sight.

A butterfly stumbles, but who cares?
It lands on a bubble, laughs with flair!
Nature joins in this merry affair,
With whispers of joy that tickle and flare.

The day fades gently, soft as a sigh,
While stars peek down from the velvet sky.
Together we giggle, with spirits so bright,
In this fancy world, everything's just right.

Dappled Light on Water's Edge

On the bank, shadows twist and twirl,
Where the shimmering lily pads swirl.
Giggling minnows race in line,
Winking at sunbeams, feeling fine.

The breeze flirts with the dragonflies,
As they spin and whirl under moonlit skies.
Tadpoles wear tiny, sparkling caps,
Leaping for fun, sneaky little chaps.

While nearby, a duck takes a dive,
With an elegant splash, it brings a jive.
A chorus of chuckles from frogs anew,
Join nature's band, in joyful view.

Laughter echoes along the rim,
As we join in with each joyful whim.
In dappled light, we chase and play,
In this merry place, we'll forever stay.

Ethereal Drops and Whimsical Winds

In the morning, raindrops tumble down,
Painting the world in a sparkly gown.
Dancing flowers with a giggle or two,
Wink at the clouds, all fluffy and blue.

Cuties in puddles begin to leap,
While ants in hats march past in a sweep.
The river chuckles, splashes galore,
Sprinkling joy from its laughing core.

A breeze tickles giggling leaves high,
As they flit about, oh my, oh my!
Circling streams weave tales so bright,
With tipsy tricks, a playful sight.

So join this dance, let laughter ring,
As each tiny droplet starts to sing.
In this enchanted, cheerful air,
The world rejoices, beyond compare.

Ethereal Moments

Floating whims like cotton candy,
Dancing in the sun's embrace,
Giggles ride the gentle breeze,
As laughter finds its perfect place.

Wobbly vessels, bright and round,
Chasing shadows on the grass,
Each pop brings a joyful sound,
Time slips by, too quick to last.

Silly shapes in merry flight,
Kicking clouds with playful cheer,
Every burst a tiny delight,
Life's a game, so crisp and clear.

In the air, a fest of dreams,
Tickled by a sunlight beam,
Chasing joy, or so it seems,
Every moment, just a gleam.

Vibrant Dreams in Morning Mist

Glimmers wink from dew-kissed grass,
Whirls of giggles in the air,
Teasing whispers as they pass,
A joyful dance without a care.

Popping colors, bright and bold,
Skimming like a playful kite,
Stories of the day unfold,
In laughter's warm and cozy light.

Chasing trails of swirling fun,
Squiggles painting blissful skies,
Every twirl, a hopeful run,
In a world that's full of lies.

Morning's glow, a chuckle's grace,
Beneath the mist, mischief sways,
Life's a dream, a silly race,
Filled with giggles, glow, and rays.

Traces of Radiance

Wobbly wonders float above,
Glinting in a cheeky light,
Chasing joy with push and shove,
As dogs bark and children bite.

Twists and twirls with shining shouts,
Romping through the sunny air,
Silly games without any doubts,
Each laugh is a delightful fare.

Colors splatter, rise and dip,
Zooming through the azure height,
Every sniff, a joyful trip,
Radiance, oh what a sight!

Chasing dreams on a whimsy path,
Witty giggles on parade,
Every moment math with laughter,
In this game we all have played.

The Art of Transience

Sailing softly, light as air,
Quirky whispers swirl and glide,
Painting joy, free from care,
In this dance, we take a ride.

Every rise holds tales unknown,
Squiggles wink, a cheeky tease,
In their flight, a laugh is sown,
Fleeting moments, bound to please.

With a tug, they shift and sway,
In this circus of delight,
Laughter carries them away,
Bubbling through the starry night.

Lively moments worth the chase,
Dancing dreams we can't replay,
In the joy of fleeting grace,
We find bliss in the fray.

www.ingramcontent.com/pod-product-compliance
Lightning Source LLC
Chambersburg PA
CBHW070007300426
43661CB00141B/330